SCOTCH WHISKY
TOP SINGLE MALTS

Doug McIvor

PRC

This edition first published in 1998 by
PRC Publishing Ltd,
Kiln House, 210 New Kings Road, London SW6 4NZ
exclusively for Chapters in Canada

ISBN 1 85648 465 3

Printed and bound in Hong Kong
Reprinted 1999

This book has been written in association with Milroy's of Soho Ltd., 3
Greek Street, London W1V 6NX. Milroy's are renowned for their huge
selection of 500 whiskies from around the world and can be contacted
on 44 (0)171 437 9311 (phone); 44 (0)171 437 1345 (fax).

Acknowledgements

Much of the information I have gathered over the years has resulted from
the daily tussle of life as a whisky salesman, be it talking to customers—
some surprisingly well-versed in the subject—visiting distilleries or deal-
ing with suppliers, who have helped enormously.

There are too many people to thank individually, but two men—John
and Wallace Milroy—have been an inspiration to me throughout my
career.

I must also give credit to Bridget Arthur and John Scott (both of
Milroy's) for their patience; Richard Brown (Matthew Gloat and Son
Ltd.), Alice Challard (Campbell Distillers), Roger Mallandine and Graeme
Tulloch (United Distillers), Richard Mallinson (Mentzendorff and Co.),
George Bevans (Morrison-Bowmore Distillers). The photographs in the
Introduction are courtesy Matthew Gloat and Son Ltd.

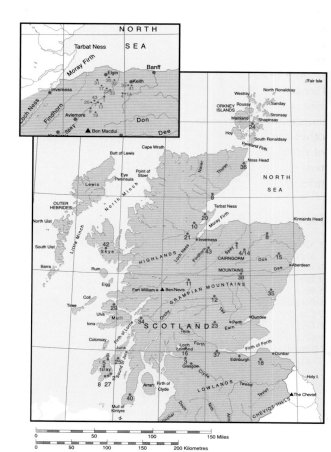

Introduction

It was not my intention when writing this book to produce the definitive work on Scotch whisky: there are already many excellent volumes which give very detailed accounts of the history, production and appreciation of this noble drink. Instead, I have attempted to define succinctly for the purpose of those beginning their journey into the realm of malts, much useful information about the whisky, the main methods of production, together with a guide providing locations, status, background history, and tasting notes, for many of the great malts.

I have included a section which explains how to obtain the greatest pleasure from drinking malts. I am often asked, "How much water should I add?" or "Should I add ice?" These questions are answered together with tips on how to evaluate a malt by assessing its components to help you to understand each part of the whole flavor sensation.

The malts featured in this book have been chosen to display the full spectrum of flavors available, and many are perfect reflections of their regions' traditional style. Suggestions are also made as to their suitability—as either an aperitif or digestif whisky.

At this point I must apologise to the distillers (Scottish or otherwise) of many excellent malts whose products do not feature in these pages. I sincerely hope that the reader is enthused to try other malts in due course and I have listed many of the other distilleries on page 96. There are currently fewer working distilleries around Scotland than hitherto; others are temporarily closed (or

Key to map (page numbers in brackets)

mothballed) and sadly some have closed their doors for good. Stocks of whisky from this latter category are dwindling, so I would urge you to try these—if you can—before they disappear forever. Most of the more unusual whiskies can be found through specialist independent bottlers.

Happily, though, the malts featured in the guide section are generally mainstream bottlings and available widely at the time of writing. It is my hope that you will seek out these superb whiskies and, with this guide to hand, begin to explore the complexities of this precious liquid which is *uisge beathe*—the water of life.

THE SINGLE MALT SCOTCH WHISKY

Scotland's single malts have for too long been eclipsed by their more heavily marketed cousins, the blended whiskies. I am very partial to a Famous Grouse, a J&B or a Chivas Regal; in fact, I find the entire world of whiskies a fascinating and enjoyable subject.

Scotland has a unique geography and climate, ideally suited to whisky making; pretenders to the throne have tried to replicate her product but failed. The Japanese distillers eventually adopted an "if you can't match them, buy them" philosophy to Scottish distilleries when their own attempts fell short of expectations.

What makes single malts so special? Three words come to mind—quality, personality, and diversity—and a fuller story emerges as you experience each new style. Single malts have individuality; each has its own unique presence and is

uncannily good at reflecting the environment in which it was distilled and matured. These factors, and the diversity of available flavors, make malt drinking immensely pleasurable.

Just as each malt tastes different, each distillery set up is different. Most have an exclusive water source; their owners have individual preferences for the type of barley they buy and the amount of peat smoke they allow to infuse the grain. But the most profound influence, determining the body and soul of a malt whisky, is the size and shape of the pot stills used to make it. As a rule, small stills give heavier, oily spirit and the larger types give lighter results.

MALT IN THE MAKING
Early illicit distillers who used crude, concealable stills or "black pots" would wonder at the sophistication of modern techniques and machinery. Yet the principles of whisky-making have changed little, and many features of today's distilleries betray more primitive origins.

Malting
Barley is steeped in bins for around three days before being spread on a malting floor. The grain is turned either by hand or mechanically to maintain an even temperature which promotes germination and the release of natural sugars. Next the barley is kiln-dried to prevent over-germination. It is spread out on a mesh platform under which a peat fire burns, and smoke is allowed to permeate the grains to a specified degree. The resulting intensity of "peat reek" can be detected in the finished whisky.

Mashing
The malted barley is milled, the resulting "grist" mixed with water in a mash tun (large tank), and stirred until the sugars break down to produce a sweet liquid called "wort."

Fermentation
Wort is transferred into washbacks (cylindrical tanks with lids) and yeast is added as a catalyst to trigger fermentation. Some hours later, a light beer called "wash" results.

Distillation
Wash is "cleaned up" in the first (wash) still to produce stronger "low wines," which are collected and passed through the spirit still for further refinement. The heated stills cause their liquid contents to vaporize upwards to the swan-shaped neck where condensation occurs, and spirit is drawn off. There are normally two stills working in tandem,

and when they reach optimum temperature the best spirit is produced.

The stillman decides at which point the required spirit is flowing, and diverts it by remote means through a spirit safe to cask (only the exciseman has direct access to the spirit via padlock and key!). The unwanted first and last cuts of each run ("foreshots" and "feints") are separated and returned to the wash still for reprocessing.

Maturation

After three years—warehoused in oak cask—the spirit can officially be called Scotch whisky. Each cask differently flavors its contents: it may previously have held bourbon or sherry for example, and as it sleeps the spirit breathes surrounding air losing some volume and strength. This percentage is the "angels' share." Malts average 12 years in wood before they are considered mature enough to bottle.

THE PRODUCING REGIONS

Some regions have a recognizable style, but it is unwise to over-generalize for there are frequent exceptions.

Lowlands

Despite associations with grain whisky, this region retains a handful of singles, separated from their Highland cousins by an imaginary line which runs from Clydeside north-eastwards to Dundee. Lowland malts are light and dry compared to others, and can be enjoyed as aperitifs.

Southern Highlands

Fuller, mostly sweeter than Lowlanders, yet by no means the biggest Highlanders. Distilleries are easily reached from Glasgow and Edinburgh; a trail which takes in the beauty of Loch Lomond, the Trossachs and Perthshire.

Western Highlands

This area has only two surviving distilleries. The town of Oban is the gateway to the Western Isles and its distillery sits in the high street. Ben Nevis, which lies in the shadow of its famous namesake-mountain, is Japanese-owned and is Fort William's only remaining distillery.

Speyside

Scotland's "Golden Triangle" of concentrated production: Speyside's salmon rivers are lined by a host of famous distilleries—Glenlivet, Glenfiddich, and Macallan, to name just three of its legendary malts. The demand for The Glenlivet malt was such that several surrounding distillers adopted its

Above: Whisky maturing in sherry casks at Mcallan's.

name as a suffix to their own, though some are now confident enough of their whiskies to have discontinued this practice. Some outlying distilleries, which spread northward to Elgin or eastward to Keith and beyond, are included as Speysiders. The malts are capable of great subtlety and complexity, sometimes spicy, sweet and floral with restrained smoke.

Eastern Highlands

A scattering of distilleries lie to the south-east of Speyside and up the North Sea coast from Montrose to Banff. These East Highland malts include some great after-dinner drams, although there is no particular regional style.

Northern Highlands

A good tank of fuel and an abstemious driver would be helpful if you wish to enjoy the hospitality of these far-flung distilleries. The area stretches from Dalwhinnie in Strathspey, northward past Inverness, taking in amongst others the famous Glenmorangie distillery at Tain. The trail ends at Wick, where the mainland's most northerly malt, Old Pulteney, is produced. A wide variety of styles can be tried including some salty coastal examples.

Islands

There are five producing islands—not including Islay which has earned its own appellation. Arran has a new set-up at Lochranza and the whisky already promises to be good. Jura lies just north of Islay: its malt is light for an Islander. Mull and Skye each have a distillery, and even the remote Orkneys have a distilling heritage. Highland Park at Kirkwall is one of the greats and readily available, whereas. Scapa is now closed and harder to find in bottle. The Islanders fall between Highland and Islay in style.

Islay

Islay stands apart from other regions—its whiskies are much peatier in style, and because the distilleries all have coastal locations, there is an inbuilt marine quality about them. Seven distilleries are able to produce, there would be eight, but for the closure of Port Ellen in 1984. It is now a malting center, supplementing the requirements of other distilleries.

The south-shore malts are fuller-peated, medicinal and intense. The legendary Laphroaigs, Lagavulins and Ardbegs can be too much for some palates, so for a gentler introduction try Bunnahabhain or Bowmore.

Campbeltown

Campbeltown is situated on Scotland's famous south-western peninsula, the Mull of Kintyre. It was once an important hub of distilling with over 30 operations, but reputations suffered when some producers cut quality to satisfy high demand and many closures followed. Only two distilleries still survive to keep the flag flying.

TUNING IN TO SINGLE MALTS

I enjoy my dram most at the end of a hard day when the armchair beckons and, with glass in hand, I close my eyes and sip. Naturally, we all have our own rituals and occasions when a glass simply hits the spot. There is, however, a more analytical approach to appreciating the complexities of malt whisky and although you may not always wish to be thinking while drinking, it is useful to learn the method and can be great fun.

Above: Casks at Bunnahabhain Distillery.

Our senses of smell and taste combine to tell us much about single malts. The taste buds perceive salt, sweet, bitter and sour flavors but our olfactory or nasal senses are more highly developed and capable of identifying over 30 primary aromas.

There exists, in addition to the single malt whisky, a single-single variety which is not only the product of one distillery, but has been selected from an individual cask. These are often bottled at "cask strength," and it is not unusual to find examples in excess of 57 percent alcohol, leaving the consumer to dilute the whisky to a preferred drinking strength.

Nosing and Tasting Procedure

Step 1: Use your eyes. Assess the color of the whisky. Is it light or dark? If dark, it may be sherried, or could be more mature than an average aged malt. Swirl the malt around a bit, and look for "legs"—these appear like tears on the side of the glass. A malt which has good legs will be oilier in body.

Step 2: Nose the whisky lightly to ascertain the more prominent aromas. Add a little water and try again. The water should kill some alcohol and unlock the whisky's aromatics: it should now be easier to identify compounds and background nuances should show through.

Step 3: Take a mouthful. Different parts of the mouth detect different flavors so coat the whole mouth before swallowing. Try to evaluate the initial flavors, the mouth-feel of the whisky, and finally, assess the finish—is it long, short, dry, sweet, and so on, and which other flavors accompany it?

Some Do's and Don'ts

• Do use a fluted glass, preferably tulip-shaped so that the aromatics or "volatiles" can be concentrated around the nose.

• Do add good quality spring water (still) but reduce the whisky carefully so as not to drown it. Some sherried whiskies cannot take much water. Avoid using tap water which is hard or heavily treated with chlorine/fluoride.

• Do drink water between whiskies to refresh the palate.

• Don't add ice to malt whisky. This will destroy the aromatics.

• Don't sniff the whisky repeatedly. Your sense of smell will soon anaesthetize, especially with high proof malts, and furthermore, it can be unpleasant.

• Don't be afraid of tasting jargon: we are all different—we perceive things differently and express things differently.

Aberlour

Region: Speyside
Map Ref: 1
Owners: Campbell Distillers Ltd.
Address: Aberlour, Banffshire, AB38 9PJ
Telephone: 44 (0)1340 871204
Status: Operational, open to visitors

Aberlour is a whisky with a "French Connection," for it is owned by the giant Pernod Ricard Group. The brand is extremely popular in France and rates in the top ten selling malts worldwide.

The first distillery at Aberlour appeared in 1826 but was destroyed by fire and most of today's Victorian structure results from rebuilding in 1880. There have been further additions and modernization this century, and a major refit was undertaken in the 1970s when the current owners acquired it.

There is a well in the grounds where St. Dunstan is said to have held baptisms. Unfortunately its holy water is not abundant enough for modern distilling requirements, and springs on the slopes of nearby Ben Rinnes are now put to use.

Aberlour malt is a regular award winner, its style is such that it is considered one of the great all-rounder whiskies. Maturation takes place in a mixture of bourbon and sherry casks.

Officially available as: 10 years, Limited, and Export bottlings

Suggested time to serve: After dinner

Tasting notes
Tasted: 10 years—40 percent
Nose: Full, slightly toffied and malty with mint and spice emerging
Palate: Full-bodied and smooth with mint, caramel and background smoke
Finish: Faultlessly clean, rounded, and long lasting

ABERLOUR

· EST⁰ 1879 ·

ABERLOUR
GLENLIVET
DISTILLERY

SPEYSIDE
MALT AGED
TEN YEARS

SINGLE HIGHLAND MALT
SCOTCH WHISKY

AGED **10** YEARS

70cl e

DISTILLED AND BOTTLED IN SCOTLAND
ABERLOUR GLENLIVET DISTILLERY CO. LTD.
ABERLOUR SPEYSIDE

40% vol
0754

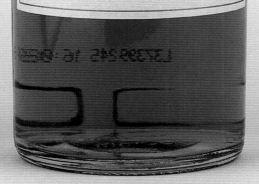

Ardbeg

Region: Islay
Map Ref: 2
Owners: Glenmorangie Plc
Address: Port Ellen, Isle of Islay, PA42 7EB
Telephone: 44 (0)1496 302418
Status: Operational, but not yet open to visitors

Ardbeg is not a whisky for the unwary. This is one of Islay's emphatic south-shore malts and is legendary to those who have come to crave Scotland's big peat-flavored drams. Maturation in proximity to the sea adds a salty-seaweedy element to this very complex spirit. The distillery is remotely situated on a rocky stretch of coastline which was once the domain of smugglers.

Ardbeg has proved popular with blenders and was owned until recently by Allied Distillers who preferred to invest money in Laphroaig, their more famous operation nearby. As a result, production at Ardbeg has been sporadic in recent years and the buildings have a neglected and haunted look, sad to see when you consider its heritage dates from the early 1800s.

The new owners, McDonald & Muir, (who also own Glenmorangie) announced in 1997 that they were going to put things right and there is even talk of restoring the traditional maltings, which once supplied the distillery with its own strongly peated barley.

A 17-year old bottling was recently launched, complemented by a limited vintage release which is heavier in style.

Officially available as: 17 years, 1974 "Provenance" cask strength, and 1978 vintage.

Suggested time to serve: After dinner

Tasting notes
Tasted: 17 years—40 percent (Distillery label)
Nose: Immediately smoky with rich brine and background sherry
Palate: Medium to full body, quite creamy and slightly nutty, then slowly drying out to reveal salt and smoke
Finish: Long, rich, and salty with a peppery finish.

ESTD 1815

Established 1815

Ardbeg

The Ultimate

SINGLE ISLAY MALT
SCOTCH WHISKY

LIMITED **1978** EDITION

BOTTLED IN THE YEAR OF 1997

ARDBEG DISTILLERY LIMITED
ISLE OF ISLAY, ARGYLL, SCOTLAND

43% vol   70 cl

Auchentoshan

Region: Lowland
Map Ref: 3
Owners: Morrison-Bowmore Distillers Ltd.
Address: Dalmuir, Dunbartonshire, G81 4SG
Telephone: 44 (0)1389 878561
Status: Operational, although not open to visitors

Auchentoshan is one of only two working distilleries in the Scottish Lowlands and is currently the only one which continues to triple-distil its whisky—once a common practice in the region.

The distillery sits on the north bank of the River Clyde near the Erskine Bridge, just a few miles downstream from Glasgow. Despite being classically Lowland in style, the whisky is made with Highland water, drawn from the Kilpatrick Hills to the north.

Records show that Auchentoshan (from old Scots, meaning "corner of the field") was founded in the early 1800s, just as Glasgow prepared for its Victorian transformation and the growth of its shipyards. The Clyde was once the world's foremost waterway and past workers at Auchentoshan could have witnessed the maiden voyages of many famous ships as they sailed down from Govan. These same shipyards were targeted heavily by German bombers during World War II, unfortunately Auchentoshan was on the flight path, and suffered badly as a consequence.

Suntory the giant Japanese distillers now own the distillery whose whisky is pleasantly light in style.

Officially available as: 10 years, 21 years, and Vintage cask strength (1965)

Suggested time to serve: Before dinner

Tasting notes
Tasted: 10 years—40 percent (Distillery label)
Nose: All sweetness and light, some citrus fruit.
Palate: Quite light and clean with a touch of oily sweetness
Finish: Appetizingly fresh, though somewhat drying

Balvenie

Region: Speyside
Map Ref: 4
Owners: Wm. Grant & Sons Ltd
Address: Dufftown, Banffshire, AB55 4DH
Telephone: 44 (0)1340 820373
Status: Operational, visitors welcome next door at Glenfiddich

Balvenie dates from 1892 and was the third distillery to be built in Dufftown; four more followed quickly and a local rhyme declares that *"Rome was built on seven hills, Dufftown was built on seven stills."*

William Grant resigned his position as manager at nearby Mortlach to start his own concern, which he named Glenfiddich; five years later he built Balvenie on adjoining farmland. His direct descendants still own both distilleries and much tradition has been maintained in the manufacture of their whiskies.

Balvenie was used primarily in the family's famous blends, and was not released as a single malt until 1973. It is fuller and richer than Glenfiddich although it shares water from the Robbie Dubh Spring along with coopering and coppersmithing facilities.

Balvenie has its own traditional floor maltings and exchanges a proportion of its grain in order to use Glenfiddich's in-house bottling services. The majority of casks used are ex-bourbon fills, and a proportion of sherrywood is used for finishing purposes. There are currently four pairs of stills *in situ*, which are heated by steam.

Officially available as: 10 years, 12 years double wood, 15 years single barrel, 21 years port finish

Suggested time to serve: After dinner

Tasting notes
Tasted: 10 years—40 percent (Distillery label)
Nose: Deep with an attractive honey-melon and brandy aroma
Palate: A slight dry prickle cuts through initial sweetness
Finish: Long and rich with some lingering sweetness

ESTᴰ 1892

SINGLE MALT

Distilled at

THE BALVENIE

Distillery, Banffshire

SCOTLAND

FOUNDER'S RESERVE
MALT SCOTCH WHISKY

AGED **10** YEARS

The Balvenie Distillery has been owned
AND MANAGED BY OUR INDEPENDENT
family company for five generations.

⟐ AT BALVENIE ⟐

there are four maltmen, three mashmen,
three tun room men, and three stillmen
AND BETWEEN THEM
they make all The Balvenie we bottle.

David Stewart

THE BALVENIE MALTMASTER

THE BALVENIE DISTILLERY COMPANY, BALVENIE MALTINGS, DUFFTOWN,
BANFFSHIRE, SCOTLAND AB55 4BB

70 cle   40% vol
PRODUCT OF SCOTLAND

Bowmore Islay

Region: Islay
Map Ref: 5
Owners: Morrison-Bowmore Distillers
Part of Suntory
Address: Bowmore, Islay, Argyll, PA43 7JS
Telephone: 44 (0)1496 810441
Status: Operational, excellent visitors' facilities including tours and shop

On my first visit to Bowmore Distillery James McEwan, then the manager, attempted to confiscate my watch. I held on to it though, because it had belonged to my father. What James was trying to do was make me forget about time and relax. He needn't have bothered—I forgot about time and missed the return ferry by a day!

Islay is a pace or two behind the mainland, in fact the only thing which runs fast is the spirit off the stills. Bowmore is the island's capital and has a distinctive round church at the top of the main drag. It was constructed in such a fashion so that the devil had no corner to hide in. At the bottom of the town near the harbor lies Bowmore Distillery which is one of Scotland's oldest (1779). This is an excellent place to visit if you want to see how whisky is made in keeping with tradition.

Bowmore's malt is not the heaviest-peated of all the Islays; it is middle-weight and approachable to novice drinkers. Bourbon and sherry maturation is preferred, although there have recently been some limited edition "Black Bowmores" of rich, mature sherry character and huge complexity. These are now scarce and expensive.

Officially available as: Unaged, 10 years, 12 years, 15 years, 17 years, 21 years, 25 years, all in bottle; 22–30 years in ceramic decanters; and a limited edition 40 years.

Suggested time to serve: Before or after dinner

Tasting notes
Tasted: 12 years—40 percent (Distillery label)
Nose: Perfumy with wavering saltiness and peat
Palate: Light- to medium-bodied with complex salt, sherry, and peat notes
Finish: Long, with salt and pepper, balanced by a hint of sherry

Bunnahabhain

Region: Islay
Map Ref: 6
Owners: Highland Distilleries Co. Plc
Address: Port Askaig, Islay, Argyll, PA46 7RR
Telephone: 44 (0)1496 840646
Status: Operational, visitors by appointment

Bunnahabhain (pronounced Boonahavan) is Islay's most secluded distillery. The name translates from the Gaelic to "Mouth of the River," referring to the Margadale which enters the Sound of Islay nearby. The distillery water is drawn from streams in the hills behind, whence there is a spectacular view over the Isle of Jura and its famous mountains—"The Paps"—so named because they are said to resemble breasts.

The central buildings of Bunnahabhain form a courtyard. The distillery dates from 1883 when the Victorian whisky boom was in full swing, and the local landowners seized the opportunity to put their barley to lucrative use. Highland Distilleries have owned the operation since 1887 and the whisky is used in The Famous Grouse, their leading blend.

Bunnahabhain is light for an Islay, but still has peaty and salty traces, although latter-day bottlings were fuller, more distinctly Islay. Bourbon and sherry casks are used for maturation and there are two sets of large onion-shaped stills functioning.

Officially available as: 12 years, 1963 limited vintage

Suggested time to serve: After dinner

Tasting notes
Tasted: 12 years—40 percent (Distillery label)
Nose: Almost apple-fresh with a hint of salt-sea air
Palate: Lightish at first, developing more body and flowery sweetness with a restrained peatiness
Finish: Pleasant and refreshing: Is one glass enough?

aged **12** years

"Westering Home"...

Bunnahabhain
SINGLE ISLAY MALT SCOTCH WHISKY

PRODUCT OF SCOTLAND
THE BUNNAHABHAIN DISTILLERY COMPANY.
BUNNAHABHAIN. ISLE OF ISLAY. SCOTLAND. BOTTLED IN SCOTLAND.

40% vol.   70 cl

Cardhu

Region: Speyside
Map Ref: 7
Owners: United Distillers
Address: Knockando, Aberlour, Banffshire, AB38 7RY
Telephone: 44 (0)1346 810204
Status: Operational, open to visitors

I have tried to resist buying a bottle of Cardhu on occasions for I know it will "evaporate" very quickly in my house—nothing to do with central heating—it is just such an approachable whisky which slides down with impeccable manners.

The distillery occupies a site on the slopes of the Mannoch Hill, not far from Aberlour, and has an intriguing history, which predates its official licensing in 1824. John Cummings, a local farmer, took a lease on land surrounding Cardhu in 1811; he then set about making illicit whisky with the help of his wife, Helen, who acted as a look-out should the exciseman come snooping. Once legitimate, Cardhu grew to be highly regarded and eventually passed into the hands of Johnnie Walker and Sons, of whose blends it has long been a key ingredient.

The Cardhu single malt (sometimes known previously as Cardow), is now a leading brand for United Distillers and is widely available. The distillery is picturesque with traditional pagoda roofs and a dam alongside. There are three sets of stills *in situ*.

Officially available as: 12 years

Suggested time to serve: After dinner

Tasting notes
Tasted: 12 years—40 percent (Distillery label)
Nose: Bewitchingly aromatic although nothing seems to dominate. Perhaps a trace of smoke with floral, honeyed notes
Palate: Medium-bodied and silky smooth, a little sweet with a subtle spiciness
Finish: Delicately peaty with some lingering sweetness

Clynelish

Region: Northern Highland
Map Ref: 8
Owners: United Distillers
Address: Brora, Sutherland, SW9 6LB
Telephone: 44 (0)1408 621444
Status: Operational, visitors by appointment

The town of Brora is situated on the eastern coast of Sutherland, a county which is often referred to as "Britain's last great wilderness." Brora's first distillery appeared in 1819 when the Marquis of Stafford (later to become Duke of Sutherland) built the Clynelish operation, drawing its water from the nearby Clynemilton Burn. In the 1960s a modern distillery was constructed across the road from Clynelish (pronounced Cline-Leesh). The new complex took the Clynelish name, the original became Brora Distillery and continued to produce alongside until fairly recently. Although the original set-up produced a heavier-peated whisky, there are similarities between the two styles, notably a pronounced coastal salt flavor which is unusually heavy for the region.

Clynelish (in either guise) is highly regarded as a connoisseurs' dram, often mistaken for an Islander, but distinctive in its own way. There are six sets of stills at the modern operation, and the old distillery is being considered for use as a museum in the future.

Officially available as: 14 years, 1982 cask strength, and 24 years Rare Malts cask strength

Suggested time to serve: After dinner

Tasting notes
Tasted: 14 years—43 percent (Distillery label)
Nose: Fresh and salty, peaty, and faintly smoky
Palate: Quite full at first, becoming drier as the smokiness develops
Finish: Long complex and peppery. Very flavorsome

CASK STRENGTH

CLYNELISH

HIGHLAND SINGLE MALT
SCOTCH WHISKY

YEAR OF DISTILLATION

1982

LIMITED BOTTLING

BOTTLED IN 1997

57.7%vol   70cle

Distilled & Bottled in *SCOTLAND*
Clynelish Distillery, Brora, Sutherland, *Scotland*

This complex and lively Northern Highland malt has a seaside nose shrouded with peat. Best enjoyed with the addition of water, it is sweet and fresh with a long finish of sweet fruits and scented smoke.

Distilled in 1982
This limited bottling, direct from the cask, has the natural strength achieved at maturation. Bottled in 199

BOTTLE NUMBER

00787

Cragganmore

Region: Speyside
Map Ref: 9
Owners: United Distillers
Address: Ballindalloch, Banffshire, AB37 9AB
Telephone: 44 (0)1807 500202
Status: Operational, not open to visitors

Cragganmore features as one of United Distillers "Classic Six" malt range, representing the Speyside style with great panache. The label on each bottle depicts a steam train puffing its way from the distillery—recollecting the railroad which once carried casks off along the banks of the River Spey.

The founder of Cragganmore (in 1869), John Smith, was a large character (weighing about 300lb.) who had deep associations with distilling. His resumé was already impressive by the time he came to Cragganmore and his father (or so it is believed), George Smith, owned The Glenlivet Distillery just five miles away. The Cragganmore Distillery is thought to have been the first to be positioned to take advantage of the railroad and Smith made full use of the facility by building his own sidings. It is said that he was a great railway buff, although his bulk excluded him from using the carriages and he had to slum it in the guards van!

There are two sets of stills at Cragganmore, which have an unusual flat-topped appearance and it is thought that this helps bring about a lightness in the whisky. The malt is associated with White Horse blends and is a component of McCallum's bblended whisky which is prominent in Australasia.

Officially available as: 12 years

Suggested time to serve: After dinner

Tasting notes
Tasted: 12 years—40 percent (Distillery label)
Nose: One to ponder over; extremity has traces of pine, spice, and sweet apples. A little smokiness is evident
Palate: Peppery dryness develops to a fuller-bodied, malty sweetness
Finish: The finish is reasonably long if a little dry.

YEARS **12** OLD

DISTILLERY CRAGGANMORE BALLINDALLOCH

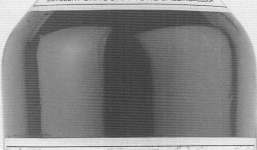

The Best of Speyside

MALT

CRAGGANMORE

SINGLE HIGHLAND MALT

AGED **12** YEARS

Scotch Whisky

AN *ELEGANT, SOPHISTICATED* SPEYSIDE with the most
complex aroma of any malt. Astonishingly fragrant with
sweetish notes and a smoky maltiness on the finish.

40%vol   70cl e

SPECIALLY BOTTLED IN SCOTLAND FOR THE
CRAGGANMORE DISTILLERY, BALLINDALLOCH, BANFFSHIRE

Dalmore

Region: Northern Highland
Map Ref: 10
Owners: Whyte & Mackay Group Plc
Address: Alness, Ross-shire, IV17 0UT
Telephone: 44 (0)1349 882362
Status: Operational, visitors by appointment

Dalmore is situated on a gentle stretch of shoreline on the Cromarty Firth, facing across the water to the Black Isle. The surrounding countryside is of rolling hills, woodland, charming Highland villages, and the nearby town of Alness, which gives its name to the river from which the distillery takes water. Dalmore Distillery was built in 1839 on farmland bought by Alexander Matheson, a wealthy tea and opium trader, and was let to the Mackenzie family who were his tenants. Eventually the Mackenzies were able to buy the distillery and retained ownership until 1960 when they joined forces with Whyte & Mackay. The stag's head, which appears on the Dalmore label, is the badge of the Mackenzie Clan and is a reminder of the malt's heritage.

The distillery is equipped with eight stills, four dating from 1966 when much work was carried out, and the spirit stills are cooled by rather unusual water jackets. Maturation is mainly in bourbon wood, although everything is vatted into sherry butts for finishing.

Officially available as: 12 years

Suggested time to serve: After dinner

Tasting notes
Tasted: 12 years—40 percent (Distillery label)
Nose: Intensely fruity; chocolate-orange, and sherry
Palate: Rounded and satisfying with some gentle smokiness, plus a little spicy prickle
Finish: Becoming dry, but extremely moreish

THE

DALMORE™

SINGLE
HIGHLAND MALT
SCOTCH WHISKY

AGED **12** YEARS

70cl

THE DALMORE DISTILLERY SCOTLAND
DISTILLED, AGED & BOTTLED
IN SCOTLAND

40%vol

Dalwhinnie

Regional: Northern Highland
Map Ref: 11
Owners: United Distillers
Address: Dalwhinnie, Inverness-shire, PH19 1AB
Telephone: 44 (0)1528 522240
Status: Operational, open to visitors

Dalwhinnie is not the sort of place you want to break down in winter: the wind howls, the roads are often blocked with snow, and the air is too pure for my London lungs. To get there, leave the A9, Perth to Inverness road, and climb up into the Grampian Mountains. By the Pass of Drumochter you will eventually reach a little transport café which once provided me with a good plate of sausage, egg, and chips. Just across the road lies Dalwhinnie distillery, where I could have sampled an excellent aperitif malt whisky if the cooking smells had not got to me first. I tried a dram anyway. At over 1,000ft. above sea level this is one of Scotland's highest distilleries and the purity of air and water seem to translate into the whisky itself. The distillery was originally christened Strathspey; its modern name means "meeting place" in Gaelic, making reference to historical associations with the cattle drovers who would camp here before moving onto the lower market towns.

The blending firm Buchanan's has used Dalwhinnie malt over the years in its Black & White brand, although the single malt is now part of United Distillers' heavily promoted classic malts portfolio, and is deservedly reaching a larger audience. The distillery output is quite small as there is only a single set of stills in use.

Officially available as: 15 years

Suggested time to serve: Before dinner

Tasting notes
Tasted: 15 years—43 percent (Distillery label)
Nose: Invitingly gentle, with a little peat and a little pear juice
Palate: Not an altogether lightweight, but well balanced, developing a heather-honey character
Finish: Long and honeyish with a hint of peat smoke

The Edradour

Region: Southern Highland
Map Ref: 12
Owners: Campbell Distillers Ltd.
Address: Pitlochry, Perthshire, PH16 2JP
Telephone: 44 (0)1796 473524
Status: Operational, open to visitors

Edradour and its big sister Aberlour (Speyside—see page 10) are French-owned by the giant drinks group Pernod Ricard. However, when you visit Edradour there is little evidence of global marketing. This distillery is Scotland's smallest, employing just three people at the last count, and it is a must to visit if you wish to see whisky being made in the original cottage craft fashion.

Distilling began in 1825 and there have been very few alterations to the formula in Edradour's history. The stills employed are the smallest the law permits. It is said that smaller stills are too easily concealed and might encourage some illicit DIY. The size of her stills, and the fact that there are but two, results in extremely limited output, just a dozen casks a week at Edradour, or about one-fiftieth of average annual output elsewhere.

Most of the malt is now bottled as a single and a little finds its way into Campbell Distillers' blends. Sherry casks are filled for maturation, the olorosse type being preferred, but the flavor does not overwhelm the whisky.

Officially available as: 10 years

Suggested time to serve: Before or after dinner

Tasting notes
Tasted: 10 years—40 percent (Distillery label)
Nose: Almost heady; nutty with honeysuckle and whiffs of sherry
Palate: Quite oily and layered, with a nutty, minty-sweetness
Finish: A little spicy then becoming drier

**THE
EDRADOUR**

EST. 1825

*The smallest distillery
in Scotland*

70cl   40%vol

*Single Highland Malt
Scotch Whisky*

GLENFORRES-GLENLIVET DISTILLERY CO. LTD.
EDRADOUR DISTILLERY, PITLOCHRY, SCOTLAND

PRODUCT OF SCOTLAND

Glenfarclas

Region: Speyside
Map Ref: 13
Owner: J. & G. Grant Ltd.
Address: Marypark, Ballindalloch, Banffshire, AB37 9BD
Telephone: 44 (0)1807 500245
Status: Operational, excellent facilities for visitors

Glenfarclas is one of Scotland's "Rolls-Royce" malt whiskies and, fittingly enough, it is a regular stop-off for vintage car rallies. It is owned and operated by the Grant family, the present managing director, being John Grant, the great-great-grandson of his namesake, who bought the distillery in 1865. The distillery was leased to John Smith (of Cragganmore fame) for five years until the Grant Association began properly in 1870.

Glenfarclas has the largest stills in Speyside, and for most of its long history made do with one set. Water for the distillery runs down from springs on the slopes of mighty Benrinnes, and its purity has much to do with the whisky's excellence. Much modernization has occurred in recent years, there now being six stills—two were added in 1960, two more in 1976—and all are exact replicas of the originals. The stills are gas-fired which is unusual today.

Glenfarclas single malt is available in a range of ages, with my personal favorite being the robust 15-year old, but having said that, I have never turned down a glass of any age or strength.

Officially available as: 10 years, 15 years, 21 years, 25 years, 30 years, "105 proof" cask bottling and specials

Suggested time to serve: After dinner

Tasting notes
Tasted: 15 years—46 percent (Distillery label)
Nose: A beautifully balanced rich aroma of sherry and smoke, gentle woodiness and biscuity malt
Palate: Rich and malty with plenty of sherry which partly subsides to allow some spice and smoke to show
Finish: Rich, long and smooth

Glenfiddich

Region: Speyside
Map Ref: 14
Owner: Wm. Grant & Sons Ltd.
Address: Dufftown, Keith, Banffshire, AB55 4DH
Telephone: 44 (0)1340 820373
Status: Operational, open to visitors

Glenfiddich has won many friends since it became available as a single malt in the 1960s. Its owners, Wm. Grant & Sons, were the first to seriously attack the established blended whisky market, aiming their product at the de luxe sector. The brand has a unique position—able to mix with leading blends and yet respected as a malt by even experienced drinkers. Glenfiddich has a light style, which suits many palates and is regarded as a good introduction to single malts. I was once fortunate enough to try a 50-year old Glenfiddich and, I must admit, I found it an excellent introduction to 50-year olds.

Glenfiddich is a large distillery with 28 stills and its visitors can observe every function of whisky making, from barley to bottling. The first spirit ran from Glenfiddich's stills way back on Christmas Day 1887, after the founder, William Grant, had rescued much of the distilling apparatus from the newly refitted Cardhu Distillery. Grant soon found ready markets for his whisky, but was dealt a blow when his best customers, the Pattison Blending Company, failed in 1898. A determined individual, he nevertheless launched his own "Standfast" blend which helped to secure the success and independence of the family company to this day.

Officially available as: Special reserve, 15 years single cask, occasional specials and export bottlings

Suggested time to serve: Before or after dinner

Tasting notes
Tasted: No age given—40 percent (Distillery label)
Nose: Invitingly fresh with a touch of floral sweetness
Palate: Easy though not uncomplex, with a balance of dryness and sweetness
Finish: Some lingering sweetness plus a little peatiness

Glen Garioch

Region: Eastern Highland
Map Ref: 15
Owner: Morrison-Bowmore Distillers Ltd.
Address: Old Meldrum, Inverurie, Aberdeenshire, AB51 0ES
Telephone: 44 (0)1651 872706
Status: Non-operational, not open to visitors

Glen Garioch (pronounced Glen Geery) was founded 200 years ago. It is situated near the village of Old Meldrum, some 20 miles north-west of Aberdeen, in an area of rich farmland which is sometimes called "The Granary of Aberdeenshire." Just 10 miles from Glen Garioch lies the Pitsligo Moss from which the distillery cuts its peat. Glen Garioch operates its own maltings and peat-smoke is very evident in the whisky. Despite abundant peat and barley, the distillery once had a shortage of water, prompting The Distillers Company Ltd., (who acquired the operation in 1937) to close it in 1968. Two years later, however, Glasgow merchants Stanley P. Morrison bought Glen Garioch and created a fresh water supply by sinking a deep well in a nearby field.

The two-still set-up has now been increased to four, although the distillery is presently mothballed. Glen Garioch has two sisters—Auchentoshan (see page 14) and Bowmore (see page 18)—all three are now owned by a subsidiary of Suntory, the Japanese distilling giant.

Officially available as:
1984, 12 years, 15 years, 21 years, and limited 1968 single cask bottlings

Suggested time to serve: After dinner

Tasting notes
Tasted: 15 years—43 percent (Distillery label)
Nose: Pleasant and quite forward with peat smoke. A little flowery
Palate: Quite full bodied with immediate smokiness and some background citrus notes
Finish: Long and smooth, with some lasting wood-smoke

AGED FIFTEEN YEARS

GLEN®
GARIOCH

HIGHLAND
Single Malt
SCOTCH WHISKY

DISTILLED & BOTTLED IN SCOTLAND

70cl ℮

MORRISON'S GLEN GARIOCH DISTILLERY
OLD MELDRUM
ABERDEENSHIRE SCOTLAND

43%Vol

Distilled in the valley of the Garioch,
traditionally one of the finest
barley growing areas
in Scotland

AGED FIFTEEN YEARS

Glengoyne

Region: Southern Highland
Map Ref: 16
Owners: Lang Brothers Ltd.
Address: Dumgoyne, Stirlingshire, G63 9LB
Telephone: 44 (0)1360 550229
Status: Operational, open to visitors

First known as Burnfoot, later Glenguin, and nowadays Glengoyne, this pretty distillery has been around since 1833. It is set in a glen at the foot of the Campsie Fells, just to the north of Glasgow. The original Burnfoot name refers to a small stream which runs off the side of Dumgoyne Hill and cascades from a height of 59ft. (18m.) into a pool behind the distillery. Glengoyne is a small but neat and tidy distillery, producing a whisky which, although light for a Highlander, narrowly avoids Lowlander status, being situated just north of the dividing line. The distillery was remodeled in the late 1960s by longtime owners Lang Brothers, when a third still was added.

Much of the production process can be seen in one room, giving the visitor a nutshell explanation of distilling technique. There are three stills, one wash and two spirit, arranged to slowly produce a high quality spirit which, uniquely for scotch whisky, contains no peat traces. The younger versions of Glengoyne can be good pre-dinner drams, whereas more mature stocks have greater body and depth.

Officially available as: 10 years, 17 years, and regular vintage releases

Suggested time to serve: Before or after dinner

Tasting notes
Tasted: 10 years—40 percent (Distillery label)>
Nose: Light, fresh, and slightly fruity
Palate: Still lightish but with some oily sweetness
Finish: Drying a little, but nicely balanced

unpeated malt, lighter
and wonderfully smooth
remarkably fruity finish.

YEARS OLD
10

THE UNPEATED MALT
FROM THE SOUTHERN HIGHLANDS

PRODUCT OF SCOTLAND

BY APPOINTMENT TO H.M.   SCOTCH WHISKY DISTILLERS
QUEEN ELIZABETH THE QUEEN MOTHER   LANG BROTHERS LIMITED, GLASGOW

GLENGOYNE

SINGLE HIGHLAND MALT
SCOTCH WHISKY

DISTILLED MATURED & BOTTLED BY
LANG BROTHERS LIMITED
DUMGOYNE SCOTLAND

THE OLD 'GLEN GUIN'

*In the quiet, secluded glen
beneath the Hill of Dumgoyne,*
GLENGOYNE DISTILLERY
*captures the essence of the
soft air and the cool Glengoyne
burn water that flows into Loch
Lomond to craft this unpeated
malt Scotch whisky.*

70 cl   40% vol

*I guarantee that this malt whisky
has lain maturing in oak casks for
at least TEN years.*

Ian Taylor
DISTILLERY MANAGER

SINCE
1833

Glen Grant

Region: Speyside
Map Ref: 17
Owner: The Seagram Company Ltd.
Address: Rothes, Morayshire, AB38 7BS
Telephone: 44 (0)1542 783318
Status: Operational, open to visitors

An image on every bottle of Glen Grant depicts its tartan-clad founders—the brothers James and John Grant—supporting a cask of their whisky (or vice versa). The Grants began their operation near Rothes in 1840 and soon found success. James, the elder, became Provost of Elgin before passing his business at Glen Grant to his son, Major James Grant. The major developed the distillery, later adding a No. 2 complex which became known as Caperdonich. In 1952 Glen Grant was merged with The Glenlivet Distillery and the association remains today, although both have been absorbed by the internationally famed Seagram empire.

Glen Grant has a whisky chateau feel, with extensive gardens which were landscaped by Major James Grant. He also took trouble to install a whisky safe in the garden wall so that he could dispense hospitality as he showed visitors around. The practice is kept up today and the guests' whisky can be cut with water from a handy burn which runs alongside. The malt can be found in mature bottlings from vintage distillations dating back to the 1930s, although the five-year old is Italy's No. 1 selling malt.

Officially available as: Unaged, 10 years, 5 years (for Italy), and many older vintages from Gordon & MacPhail

Suggested time to serve: Before or after dinner (depending on age)

Tasting notes
Tasted: 10 years—40 percent (Distillery label)
Nose: Floral and cereal notes, a touch dry
Palate: A fairly light character with some biscuity dryness
Finish: Quite quick, and dry, with faint green tinges

Glenkinchie

Region: Lowland
Map Ref: 18
Owners: United Distillers
Address: Pencaitland, East Lothian, EH34 5ET
Telephone: 44 (0)1875 340333
Status: Operational, open to visitors

Glenkinchie is situated near the village of Pencaitland not far from the main A68 road, which skirts the east cost. The distillery nestles into the gentle farmland of East Lothian some 15 miles east of Edinburgh, and is the sole producer of malt whisky in the area. The distillery was once known as Milton, and adopted its current name in 1837. For a while Glenkinchie discontinued production, until the whisky boom of the late Victorian era helped revive its fortunes. It became one of the founder distilleries of D.C.L.—now United Distillers—and the company describes its 10-year old single as "The Edinburgh Malt."

There is much for the visitor to take in, including a museum, and the distillery even has its own bowling green. The malt is typically Lowland in character and represents the region in U.D.'s Classic Six malt whisky range. Odd bottles of a "Blonde" Glenkinchie called "Jackson's Row" may be found after a recent test-marketing exercise.

Officially available as: 10 years

Suggested time to serve: Before dinner

Tasting notes
Tasted: 10 years—43 percent (Distillery label)
Nose: Fresh mown hay with a sweet and greenish tinge
Palate: Clean with a little oiliness, a pleasant grassy sweetness and fuller in the mouth than first expected
Finish: Becoming dry with a slight gingery prickle

Glenkinchie

THE EDINBURGH MALT
LOWLAND SCOTCH WHISKY

10

YEARS OLD

Glenkinchie Distillery was established in 1837 by John and George Rate. It is situated beside the Kinchie Burn in the heart of East Lothian Farmland. Over the gently rolling hills around Glenkinchie, some of the finest barley is grown.

Glenkinchie Lowland Malt Whisky has a light delicate nose and a fresh clean aroma; the finish is smooth, with a subtle hint of dryness. A truly fine distinctive Single Malt, excellent as a pre-dinner drink.

43%vol

70cl℮

DISTILLED AT THE GLENKINCHIE DISTILLERY
PENCAITLAND SCOTLAND

The Glenlivet

Region: Speyside
Map Ref: 19
Owners: The Seagram Company Ltd.
Address: Ballindalloch, Banffshire, AB37 9BD
Telephone: 44 (0)1542 783220
Status: Operational, open to visitors

The Glenlivet malt whisky barely needs an introduction, for its fame is global and its quality revered. The story started in 1823, when the Duke of Gordon, who owned land in Speyside, prompted Parliament to pass an Act which offered distillers an opportunity to become legitimate without the penalty of unfair taxation. One of the duke's tenants, a farmer and illicit distiller named George Smith, took up the offer, and bought a licence. His Glenlivet distillery—which opened a year later—was the first legitimate operation, though many soon followed suit.

Smith had more than a little trouble with threats from jealous rivals, so he bought a pair of pistols which he kept at hand for several years. They are now on display at the distillery. With the Glenlivet distillery established and business going well, it became apparent that all and sundry were using its name as a marketing tool. The Smiths acted in 1880 and secured exclusive rights to the brand name, "The Glenlivet"—although some distillers in the area are still permitted to tag Glenlivet onto their own names.

The brand has done well in the U.S. market and remains the top-selling malt, assisted by the clout of its owners, The Seagram Company.

Officially available as: 12 years, 18 years, plus many unofficial ages and vintages

Suggested time to serve: Before or after dinner

Tasting notes
Tasted: 12 years—40 percent (Distillery label)
Nose: Some beautiful floral notes intermingled with sherry and delicate spice
Palate: Extremely smooth, almost creamy, with some nut and spice apparent
Finish: Long, clean, and balanced

Glenmorangie

Region: Northern Highland
Map Ref: 20
Owners: MacDonald Martin Distilleries Plc
Address: Tain, Ross-shire, IV19 1P2
Telephone: 44 (0)1862 892043
Status: Operational, visiting by appointment

It is my unerring habit, in whichever hostelry I find myself, to cast my eye along the whisky shelf. I will nearly always find a bottle of Glenfiddich, or The Glenlivet, but I am always pleased to find a Glenmorangie up there, vying for attention with the Super-Speys. This malt is one of Scotland's great successes, holding number one place in its domestic market and now exported to every corner of the world.

Glenmorangie hails from the town of Tain in Ross-shire, and this delightful pre-prandial dram is said by the marketeers to be crafted by 16 men from the town. The whisky is renowned for its aromatic bouquet, which shines through assisted by the overall lightness of the spirit. The stills at Glenmorangie are the tallest in the Highlands: they number eight today and are modeled meticulously on their predecessors. Glenmorangie's water is also an importantly different commodity, for it is hard when most distilleries prefer a soft supply. The springs employed rise in the Tarlogie Forest—which the owners have bought as a safeguard. The distillery has a sister operation at Glenmoray in Speyside, as well as the recently acquired Ardbeg set-up on Islay.

Officially available as: 10 years, 18 years, port, sherry, and madeira finish, and recent limited claret offering. Also some occasional vintage specials

Suggested time to serve: Before dinner

Tasting notes
Tasted: 10 years—40 percent (Distillery label)
Nose: Very classy, with a delicate sweetness, some oak, leafy-spice, plus some gentle woodsmoke. Perhaps a whiff of salt?
Palate: Light but satisfying with a creamy-smooth feel. Eventually some floral spice and fruit emerge
Finish: Rounded with flashes of dryness

Glen Ord

Region: Northern Highland
Map Ref: 21
Owners: United Distillers
Address: Muir of Ord, Ross-shire, IV6 7UJ
Telephone: 44 (0)1463 870421
Status: Operational, open to visitors

Glen Ord single malt has been dangled temptingly in front of consumers under various guises. Initially it was known as "Ord" after the area in which it is produced, then changed for a spell to Glen Ordie, and is now being flashed before the TV watching population of the UK under its latest identity. This is a whisky with a bright future, not least because its label proclaims, "I shine, not burn."

The "Ord" referred to in the whisky's title is an expanse of land which stretches from the shores of the Beauly Firth inland towards the village of Muir of Ord. Even the distillery name has been changed: it was once called Muir of Ord after the nearby village, but now more logically shares the name of the product.

The region north of Inverness was once a smugglers' paradise and their illicit stills (or bothies) were numerous. Glen Ord stands on the site of one of these, and only gained legitimate status in 1838. The distillery operates its own maltings, converted in recent years to a saladin box mechanical system, although today it has been updated to a more efficient drum process. There are currently three pairs of stills in place; they can be viewed through a glass partition in the stillhouse wall. Glen Ord has been associated with Dewar's blends since the 1920s and current annual output is around 750,000 litres of spirit.

Officially available as: 12 years

Suggested time to serve: After dinner

Tasting notes
Tasted: 12 years—40 percent (Distillery label)
Nose: Deep with some malty sweetness and a faint peatiness
Palate: Quite full flavored with an orangey, spicy sweetness
Finish: Lingering and gently warming

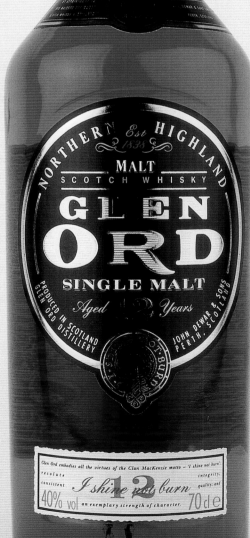

GLEN ORD DISTILLERY·
ESTABLISHED
1838 ROSS·SHIRE
THERN HIGHLAND MALT

NORTHERN Est HIGHLAND
1838
MALT
SCOTCH WHISKY
GLEN
ORD
SINGLE MALT
Aged 12 Years

PRODUCED IN SCOTLAND
GLEN ORD DISTILLERY

JOHN DEWAR & SONS
PERTH, SCOTLAND

Glen Ord embodies all the virtues of the Clan MacKenzie motto – 'I shine not burn'
resolute   integrity,
consistent   I shine not burn   quality, and
40% vol   an exemplary strength of character.   70 c l

Glenrothes

Region: Speyside
Map Ref: 22
Owners: The Highland Distilleries Co. Plc
Address: Rothes, Morayshire, AB38 7AA
Telephone: 44 (0)1340 872300
Status: Operational, not generally open to visitors

Glenrothes Distillery in the town of Rothes produced its first spirit on Sunday, December 28, 1879. The very same night, amid howling storms, a train was blown from the bridge over the River Tay near Dundee and as Scots poet extraordinaire, William McGonagall, recounts "90 lives have been taken away." The distillery flourished despite the initial ill-omen, and extensions were added in 1896. In 1922 a fire caused one of the warehouses to burn down and large quantities of mature whisky poured into the Burn of Rothes, providing a drunken feast for the locals. It was reported that even a few cows overindulged themselves. Glenrothes is made using water from a spring in the nearby Glen of Dounie. The spring is known as "the Ladies Well," after the daughter of the Earl of Rothes, who was murdered there in the fourteenth century.

Glen Rothes malt whisky is lightly peated, matured mainly in American oak and partly in sherrywood casks. Much of the product goes into the famous Cutty Sark blend, which belongs to London wine merchants, Berry Brothers & Rudd Ltd., although it is highly regarded and widely used by other blenders.

Officially available as: 1982 and 1972

Suggested time to serve: Before or after dinner

Tasting notes
Tasted: 1982 vintage—43 percent (Distillery label)
Nose: Delicate peatiness with butterscotch
Palate: Reasonably full, well balanced, with a touch of sherry and gentle spice
Finish: Long, smooth, and satisfying

THE GLENROTHES

SINGLE SPEYSIDE MALT

THE GLENROTHES DISTILLERY

SAMPLE ROOM

CHARACTER: *Ripe, fruity, vanilla notes*

CHECKED: *J. C. Stevens* DATE: *17/4/84*

APPROVED: *R. H. French* DATE: *20.8.96*

Distilled and Bottled in Scotland. Berry Bros. & Rudd, 3 St James's St, London

PRODUCT OF SCOTLAND

43% vol. 700ml

DISTILLED IN

1982

BOTTLED IN 1996

SCOTCH WHISKY

Glenturret

Region: Southern Highland
Map Ref: 23
Owners: The Highland Distilleries Co. Plc
Address: The Hosh, Crieff, Perthshire, PH7 4HA
Telephone: 44 (0)1764 656565
Status: Operational, excellent visitor center

The historic settlement of Creiff in Perthshire grew up as a cattle market town where the drovers would converge to sell their stocks. A different kind of stocks can be seen in the High Street where the less lawful or drunken folk were locked up in public view. There is evidence of distilling around the area since the early 1700s—the town's nearby Glenturret Distillery is said to have first opened in 1775, making it Scotland's oldest. For many years it was known as "the Hosh," there being another set-up in the vicinity using the Glenturret name. When this closed, the name was adopted by the existing distillery, although "the Hosh" is still referred to in its address.

Glenturret was stripped of its equipment in the lean years of the late 1920s and was not revived until 1957, when James Fairlie began to realize his dream of producing whisky in the traditional manner. Many of the procedures which are automated in modern operations are carried out by hand at Glenturret and there is a small, but much respected, output from its two stills. Glenturret is a showpiece distillery with brilliantly organised visitors' facilities, including its own bar and restaurant.

Officially available as: 12 years, 15 years, 18 years, 21 years, 15 years cask strength, and occasional vintages

Suggested time to serve: Before or after dinner (depending on age)

Tasting notes
Tasted: 12 years—40 percent (Distillery label)
Nose: Lightly toffeeish, with some dry maltiness and spice
Palate: Light but creamily smooth, and a touch of nutty dryness
Finish: Not long, but crisp and fresh, becoming dry

Highland Park

Region: Islands
Map Ref: 24
Owners: The Highland Distilleries Co. Plc
Address: Holm Road, Kirkwall, Orkney, KW15 1SU
Telephone: 44 (0)1856 873107
Status: Operational, open to visitors

The Orkney Isles have an ancient history of civilization, thought to have begun as long ago as 6,000 BC, although many of the Orcadian surnames betray the folk's Norse ancestry. The Danes and Norwegians ruled here for half a millennium before the islands were handed to King James III of Scotland in the fifteenth century.

Highland Park, at Kirkwall on the main island, is the world's most northerly distillery, with a history of legal production since 1825, although it was founded 27 years earlier by Magnus Eunson, a local smuggler-cum-preacher who is reputed to have hidden his casks in the church when the excisemen called by! Most of the equipment and processes used at Highland Park today are traditional. Peat is cut shallow from local beds and a heather-root character abides in the whisky. Occasionally sprigs of heather are thrown on the peat fire to augment the effect.

Highland Park whisky is highly regarded by blenders, having a fullness of body and a rounded enough character to help knit other whiskies together. It also has a broad appeal to the malt consumer, being one of the UK's top ten favourites and is now exported around the globe.

Officially available as: 12 years, 18 years, and 25 years at cask strength

Suggested time to serve: After dinner

Tasting notes
Tasted: 12 years—40 percent (Distillery label)
Nose: A little sherry, and some gentle, malty, spicy sweetness plus a hint of heathery peat
Palate: Medium-bodied and beautifully balanced between sweetness and smoky dryness
Finish: Impressive, heathery, with a smoky dryness

AGED **12** YEARS

ORKNEY ISLANDS

HIGHLAND PARK

SINGLE MALT SCOTCH WHISKY

ORKNEY ✦ ISLANDS

PRODUCT OF SCOTLAND

Isle of Jura

Region: Islands
Map Ref: 25
Owners: Whyte & MacKay Group Plc
Address: Craighouse, Isle of Jura, Argyll, PA60 7XT
Telephone: 44 (0)1496 820240
Status: Operational, visiting by appointment

The Sound of Jura separates this Inner Hebridean Isle from the mainland. There is one distillery here and its produce is nowhere near as peaty as that of the neighbouring Islay malt whiskies. Jura has just over 2,000 inhabitants, who share the land with a much healthier population of sheep and deer (the island takes its name from the Norse for deer). The dominant feature on Jura is "The Paps," mountains which are said to resemble a pair of breasts from certain angles, the highest peak being over 2,500ft—hardly a lady-like measurement! The writer George Orwell came to Jura in the 1940s for a bit of solitude and it was in a cottage in the northern half of the island that he wrote *1984*—his last work.

Jura Distillery has a chequered past, and was rescued and rebuilt in the 1950s and 1960s by Scottish and Newcastle Breweries distillery arm, now absorbed into the Whyte & MacKay empire. The stills at Jura are four—two wash and two spirit—and are unusually tall, a factor which is important to the lightness of the whisky. Stocks are matured in American oak casks and a smaller proportion in Olorosso sherrywood.

Officially available as: 10 years, Stillman's dram, and 26 years

Suggested time to serve: Before dinner

Tasting notes
Tasted: 10 years—40 percent (Distillery label)
Nose: Nutty and minty with a hint of caramel
Palate: Light, quite mellow with some viscosity, and a little creaminess
Finish: Subtle, though reasonably long

The Flavour of an Island

DISTILLED AND BOTTLED IN SCOTLAND
THE ISLE OF JURA DISTILLERY CO. LTD.

ISLE OF
JURA

SINGLE MALT SCOTCH WHISKY

40% vol. **AGED 10 YEARS** 70 cl

406431

Knockando

Region: Speyside
Map Ref: 26
Owners: International Distillers & Vintners Ltd.
Address: Knockando, Aberlour, Morayshire, AB38 7RD
Telephone: 44 (0)1340 810205
Status: Operational, visiting by appointment

Knockando Distillery was built by Ian Thompson in 1898, just as the whisky boom ended, and its owners soon had no choice but to halt production. They were eventually forced to sell out to Gilbeys in 1904. Gilbeys, now IDV Ltd, have retained the brand ever since, incorporating it in their popular J&B blends. Despite the negative sounding name, Knockando translates from the Gaelic for "small black hill," and because the whisky is a light style of Speyside, most palates find it will do very nicely.

Knockando is a true Speyside, situated literally a stone's throw from the river on a tree-clad bank, and although much rebuilding took place in 1969 there is still a Victorian charm about the structures. The distillery has its own pure water source at the nearby Cardnach spring. There are two sets of stills in place, and the spirit is run into American oak casks with a small amount maturing in sherrywood. The whisky is bottled when the distillery manager thinks the casks are mature, so a vintage appears on the label rather than a fixed age statement. Knockando has a sister operation, The Singleton of Auchroisk (see page 86), which is a recent distillery, situated down river near Mulben.

Officially available as: 1984, 1973 vintage in decanter

Suggested time to serve: After dinner

Tasting notes
Tasted: 1984 vintage—40 percent (Distillery label)
Nose: Sherry trifle perhaps?
Palate: Nicely balanced, a little creamy with some fruity and sherryish presence
Finish: Well mannered, and exceptionally smooth

Lagavulin

Region: Islay
Map Ref: 27
Owners: United Distillers
Address: Port Ellen, Islay, Argyll, PA42 7DZ
Telephone: 44 (0)1496 302400
Status: Operational, visiting by appointment

Islay was the stronghold of the Lords of the Isles and the ruins of their fourteenth century Dunyveg Castle overlook the entrance to Lagavulin Bay on the exposed south-eastern coast. Lagavulin means "the mill in the valley" in Gaelic, and the distillery occupies a hollow on the Kildalton shoreline. The area was a smugglers' haven in the 1740s. There are reported to have been at least ten illicit operations on the site of the modern distillery, which gives its official birth year more conservatively as 1816.

In 1867 Lagavulin came into the hands of Peter Mackie, who used its produce as the base for his now famous White Horse blend. Mackie was one of the industry's great movers and shakers, nicknamed "Restless Peter" and later knighted for his achievements. Much of his energy was concentrated at Lagavulin where he experimented with production techniques and rebuilt the old "Malt Mill" distillery, which once shared the site. He aimed to produce a traditional smugglers' style whisky. Malt Mill finally closed in the early 1960s when more room was required by Lagavulin.

Lagavulin is a hugely complex and characterful malt, which is unmistakably Islay. The maturing casks breathe the salty, seaweedy, coastal air, giving a medicinal feel to this heavily peated spirit—a great dram on a cold night. It is one of United Distillers classic six range.

Officially available as: 16 years

Suggested time to serve: After dinner

Tasting notes
Tasted: 16 years—43 percent (Distillery label).
Nose: Powerful, peaty, and medicinal with a whiff of salt and seaweed
Palate: Again powerful with a big oily body, which fattens before releasing its peaty, salty, cargo
Finish: Long and creamy becoming dry, smoky, and warming

Laphroaig

Region: Islay
Map Ref: 28
Owners: Allied Distillers Ltd.
Address: Port Ellen, Islay, PA42 7DU
Telephone: 44 (0)1496 302418
Status: Operational, visiting by appointment

I have included all three of the remaining south-shore, "Costa Del Peat and Seaweed," Islay Distilleries in this guide and, yes, I am a big fan of their whiskies. Lagavulin (see page 62), Ardbeg (see page 12), and this distinctive example, Laphroaig, are difficult to mistake as belonging to any other part of Scotland. If you cannot cope with their full-peated, medicinal flavors, then don't worry, they do take some getting use to. However, once bitten, you may be forever smitten! Laphroaig (pronounced Laffroyg) is a lighter-bodied malt whisky than its two neighbors, and as a result the peatiness shines through almost unhindered. Even the distillers confess that this is a malt you may either love or hate.

The distillery has its origins in the early 1800s and gained legal status in the hands of the Johnston family. Donald Johnston, son of the founder, gained control in 1836 and took such an interest in the distilling process that in 1847 he fell into a fermenting vat and drowned. The business continued to pass through family hands until 1954, when Mrs. Bessie Campbell took the reigns for a 16-year spell. Today, Laphroaig is owned by Allied Distillers, who have done much to promote the brand and it also features in many of their famous blends.

Officially available as: 10 years, 15 years, 10 years cask strength, and occasional vintages/older versions

Suggested time to serve: After dinner

Tasting notes
Tasted: 10 years—40 percent (Distillery label)
Nose: Peaty, smoky with iodine, and a little whiff of sherry
Palate: Reasonably full and a bit tarry. A slight oily-sweetness holds the act together nicely
Finish: Dries out quickly to leave peaty, salty, residues

LAPHROAIG®

SINGLE ISLAY MALT
SCOTCH WHISKY

10
Years Old

The most richly flavoured of
all Scotch whiskies

ESTABLISHED
1815

DISTILLED AND BOTTLED IN SCOTLAND BY
D. JOHNSTON & CO., (LAPHROAIG), LAPHROAIG DISTILLERY, ISLE OF ISLAY.

70cl   40% vol

L00717

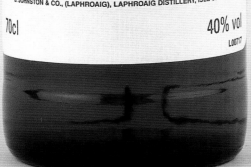

Ledaig

Region: Islands
Map Ref: 29
Owners: Burn Stewart Distillers Plc
Address: Tobermory, Mull, Argyll, PA75 6NR
Telephone: 44 (0)1688 302645
Status: Operational, open to visitors

The Isle of Mull nestles close to the rugged west coast of Scotland, its south-eastern flank facing across the Firth of Lorn to the Port of Oban where the ferries set out for the scattered Western Isles. Tobermory is Mull's principal town and fishing port, tucked into a bay to the north-east of the island where it is sheltered from the extremes of the Atlantic Ocean. The town grew up around the harbor in the late 1700s and retains its period charm today, with many of its seafront buildings painted in an array of colors which contrast with the greenery rising behind them.

A distillery was introduced in 1798 by John Sinclair, who named it Ledaig, and this name stuck until the 1970s when it was rechristened Tobermory. However for much of this time—from 1930—Ledaig's doors remained closed and did not reopen until 1972, and then only for three years. The present owners have been able to do better and now market Tobermory as an unpeated, light-ish malt together with some vintage releases of Ledaig, which retain much of its traditional peaty character. Both malts are well worth trying: Ledaig is the after dinner style, Tobermory is good at just about any time.

Officially available as: 1979 vintage; Tobermory is unaged

Suggested time to serve: Before or after dinner

Tasting notes
Tasted: Ledaig 1979 vintage—43 percent (Distillery label)
Nose: Attractively peaty with some malty sweetness and floral notes
Palate: Quite lush—syrupy—and then the peat breaks through to dry the proceedings somewhat
Finish: Good lasting roundness and Islands flavor

LEDAIG

SINGLE MALT
SCOTCH WHISKY

FROM
THE ISLE OF MULL

1979
Vintage

*This rare old single malt whisky
was distilled at the Ledaig Distillery
on the Isle of Mull by
Ledaig Distillers (Tobermory) Ltd.*

PRODUCE OF SCOTLAND

70cl   43%Vol

Linkwood

Region: Speyside
Map Ref: 30
Owners: United Distillers
Address: Elgin, Morayshire, IV30 3RD
Telephone: 44 (0)1343 547004
Status: Operational, visiting by appointment

Linkwood is beginning to achieve better recognition as a single malt: for years only the independents bothered to bottle this Speyside gem. I recently tasted a 1954 distillation put out by Elgin specialists Gordon & MacPhail, and I have to say that it is one of the most beautifully balanced and complex whiskies I have tried. Peter Brown, a local land agent and agricultural improver, built the original distillery in 1824 and named it after Linkwood House, which once occupied the wooded site.

The distillery has a cooling dam, home to a number of swans which are depicted on the label of the official 12-year old. Linkwood was rebuilt by Brown's son during the early 1870s and the buildings have changed little in outward appearance since then, despite the addition of stills in the 1960s and 1970s. There are now three sets in operation. In the 1930s Linkwood's superstitious manager, Roddy MacKenzie, was firmly of the opinion that even minute changes in the still room could affect the quality of the spirit, and with this in mind he forbade the removal even of spiders' webs. United Distillers, who own the set-up today, would rather keep the swans—outside, of course.

Officially available as: 12 years, limited edition cask strength bottlings

Suggested time to serve: After dinner

Tasting notes
Tasted: 12 years—43 percent (Distillery label)
Nose: Entrancingly fragrant with a ripe fruity sweetness, and some background floral notes. Perhaps violets?
Palate: A good body carrying some sweetness
Finish: Drying slowly to reveal a little smokiness

SPEYSIDE
SINGLE MALT
SCOTCH WHISKY

LINKWOOD

distillery stands on the *River Lossie*,
close to *ELGIN* in *Speyside*. The *distillery*
has retained its *traditional atmosphere*
since its *establishment* in 1821.
Great care &c has always
been taken to *safeguard* the
character of the *whisky* which has
remained the same through the
years. Linkwood is one of the
FINEST &c Single Malt Scotch Whiskies
available - *full bodied* with a *hint* of
sweetness and a *slightly smoky aroma*.

YEARS 12 OLD

43% vol

Distilled & Bottled in *SCOTLAND*.
LINKWOOD DISTILLERY
Elgin, Moray, *Scotland*.

70 cl

Loch Dhu

Region: Speyside
Map Ref: 31
Owners: United Distillers
Address: Elgin, Morayshire IV30 3SS
Telephone: 44 (0)1343 860331
Status: Mothballed, not open to visitors

This malt is a recent variation from a fairly recently built distillery called Mannochmore. Mannochmore malt whisky is normally unusually light in color, but the Loch Dhu version is black as sin. The color comes from double charring of the casks in which the whisky matures, a technique used in the production of bourbon, although I have never seen one this color. Charring casks was probably an accidental extension of the toasting technique used by coopers to warp the wooden staves into shape, and at some point in the mid-1800s the Americans discovered that charred wood improved the flavor of their whisky, giving it a sweeter, cleaner taste.

Loch Dhu is certainly not a normal malt whisky and it does have a background bourbon sweetness, almost liquorice-like in flavor. Mannochmore was built in 1970-71 and is classed as a River Lossie Distillery, falling into the general Speyside catchment. It is actually an annex of the Glen Lossie Distillery complex and produces only in times of heightened demand. This could mean that Mannochmore's black whisky is a fleeting experiment by United Distillers, so try it while you can.

Officially available as: 10 years; Mannochmore 12 years

Suggested time to serve: After dinner

Tasting notes
Tasted: 10 years—40 percent (Distillery label)
Nose: Almost Madeira-ised and liquorice at first then banana and toffee ice cream
Palate: Not heavy but full of flavor. Almost sour mash, and bourbon sweetness
Finish: Long, with the sweetness retreating to reveal a smoky, almost bitter finish

LOCH DHU

THE
BLACK
WHISKY

SINGLE MALT
SCOTCH

10

AGED YEARS

PRODUCT OF SCOTLAND

PRODUCED & DISTILLED BY
MANNOCHMORE
DISTILLERY
MANNOCHMORE SCOTLAND

40% VOL   70cl e

Longmorn

Region: Speyside
Map Ref: 32
Owners: The Seagram Company Ltd.
Address: Elgin, Morayshire, IV30 3ST
Telephone: 44 (0)1542 783400
Status: Operational, visiting by appointment

Longmorn is one of Speyside's great malt whiskies, golden in color, and winner of a recent gold medal in the 1994 International Wine and Spirit Challenge. It also claims the distinction of having been voted the best malt whisky in the world by the *New York Times*. They may soon have to make the warehouse doors bigger to get the ego-stricken casks out!

Production began at Longmorn in the 1890s on the site of an ancient abbey, and the name is said to be derived from "Lhanmorgund" meaning "place of the holy man." The distillery is located just south of Elgin and takes its spring water from the Mannoch Hills, which separate the Lossie and Spey Rivers. Floor maltings were suspended in 1970 but there is much of the traditional brewing and distilling equipment still in use. There are eight stills *in situ* today; much of their output is incorporated in the Chivas Brothers' blends which belong to Seagram, Longmorn's owners. Seagram own three additional distilleries in Speyside, which are marketed with Longmorn under the Heritage Selection banner, namely, Strathisla, Benriach, and Glen Keith.

Officially available as: 15 years

Suggested time to serve: After dinner

Tasting notes
Tasted: 15 years—45 percent (Distillery label)
Nose: Deep honeyish-sherried nose with some clean cereal aromas
Palate: Luscious and creamy with some nuttiness and fruit
Finish: Long, smooth, and sweet with some spirity warmth

DISTILLED AND BOTTLED IN SCOTLAND

LONGMORN

Highland Single Malt

SCOTCH WHISKY

*This outstanding single malt whisky is produced only at the
Longmorn distillery, which stands on the site of an ancient abbey,
in the heart of the Scottish Highlands.*

MATURED IN OAK CASKS
15 YEARS

70 cl   45% vol

Macallan

Region: Speyside
Map Ref: 33
Owners: the Highland Distilleries Co. Plc
Address: Craigellachie, Banffshire, AB38 9RX
Telephone: 44 (0)1340 871471
Status: Operational, visiting by appointment

If malt whiskies could be likened to rare stamps, then Macallan is surely the "Penny Black," except it is harder to lick and infinitely more pleasant to the palate. This is a class act—a big Speyside of unending complexity and moreish flavor. I once tasted a 41-year old Macallan with John Milroy and writer Jim Murray. Eventually Jim and I sloped off to a football match and at halftime I was still enjoying the Macallan's rich finish.

The distillery was licensed in 1824—the same year that The Glenlivet got going—but Macallan took much longer to make the impact of its local rival. In 1892 Macallan was purchased by Roderick Kemp, whose family had connections with the business until recently. During the 1950s a series of expansions took place, the directors taking a decision to build more stills rather than enlarging the existing type. The demand for the whisky continued to grow and, because the stills are amongst the smallest in Scotland, output was increased by adding more a few years later. There are now seven wash stills feeding 14 spirit stills.

Part of The Macallan recipe for success in recent years has been the exclusive use of dry olorosso sherry casks for maturation. It is still possible to find at auction some bottlings aged for up to 50 or 60 years in cask, but expect to pay the price of a fully fitted kitchen.

Officially available as: 10 years, 18 years, 25 years, and 7 years and 12 years for export and occasional specials

Suggested time to serve: After dinner

Tasting notes
Tasted: 10 years—40 percent; 10 years—40 percent (Distillery label)
Nose: A wave of buttery, honeyish, sherryish fragrances act as an overblanket to many other notes
Palate: Though full-bodied sherry dominates for a while until the malt and fruit emerge
Finish: Slowly drying with a stimulating pepperiness and background smoke

The Macallan

MACALLAN

MATURED IN SHERRY WOOD

PRODUCE OF   SCOTLAND

ESTABLISHED 1824

The

MACALLAN

Single Highland Malt
Scotch Whisky

YEARS 10 OLD

DISTILLED AND BOTTLED BY
THE MACALLAN DISTILLERS LTD.
CRAIGELLACHIE · SCOTLAND

40% vol   BOTTLED
IN
SCOTLAND   70 cl

Oban

Region: Western Highland
Map Ref: 34
Owners: United Distillers
Address: Stafford Street, Oban, Argyll, PA34 5NH
Telephone: 44 (0)1631 562110
Status: Operational, open to visitors

Oban is a pretty resort town and port, arranged around a busy harbor and climbing up into the hills behind. Above the town stands the coliseum-styled "McCaig's Folly," which never saw a chariot race but was commissioned as a kind of Victorian youth employment scheme to keep the local stone masons in work. Directly below it on the waterfront sits the distillery which is Scotland's only High Street operation.

Oban distillery was built by two brothers, the Stevensons, in 1794, although it took them a few years to secure a licence and it was not until the 1820s that production really got going. Towards the end of the century, new owners began to expand the distillery and while blasting into the cliff behind, the remains of Mesolithic bones were uncovered, believed to be around 4,000 years old. Dewars bought Oban in 1923, prior to the formation of the Distillers Company in 1930. Oban 14-year old is now an integral part of United Distillers' classic malts range, readily available around the world and winning many new admirers with its approachable style.

Officially available as: 14 years

Suggested time to serve: After dinner

Tasting notes
Tasted: 14 years—43 percent (Distillery label)
Nose: Quite developed with background peat-smoke, pervading an initial sweetness
Palate: Round and malty, drying as the smoke filters through
Finish: Smooth and oily at first, drying towards the end

OBAN

'Little Bay of Caves'

ALONG THE SHORES OF LORN LIES A RECORD OF
MAN FAR MORE ANCIENT THAN THAT OF ANY CITY
IN THE LAND. THE FIRST SETTLERS ARRIVED ON
THE MAINLAND IN 5,000 BC AND SHELTERED IN
THE NATURAL CAVES OF THE LAND THEN KNOWN
AS 'AN OB'. THE 'DISTILLERY CAVE' WAS ONE
SUCH SHELTER HIDDEN IN THE CREAG A' BHARRAIN
CLIFFS WHICH RISE DRAMATICALLY ABOVE THE

'OBAN DISTILLERY'

Producers of a Delicate

SINGLE MALT

WEST *Highland* MALT
SCOTCH WHISKY

OBAN DISTILLERY OBAN ARGYLL SCOTLAND

43% vol   70 cl

Old Fettercairn

Region: Eastern Highland
Map Ref: 35
Owners: Whyte & Mackay Plc
Address: Distillery Road, Laurencekirk, Kincardineshire, AB30 1YE
Status: Operational, open to visitors

This distillery lies just north of Brechin Town and a few miles inland of the North Sea. The eastern extremes of the Grampian Mountain range descend towards the village of Fettercairn, carrying pure Highland spring water to the distillery. Fettercairn was built on the Fasque Estate whose house and fertile lands once belonged to John Gladstone, father of British Liberal Prime Minster William Gladstone, who served four separate terms in office and was a useful ally of the distillers—in 1853 he abolished the malt tax, rejuvenating the industry.

Fettercairn's buildings were converted from an old corn mill in 1824 when the first licences for legal distilling were being granted. There was no shortage of local expertise as most of the farming population were well educated in the craft of whisky making. A fire destroyed the original distillery in 1887, but the demand for whisky was so great at the time, that the distillery was up and running again shortly afterwards.

The distillery fell silent in 1926 and remained so until the 1940s when Associated Scottish Distillers acquired it. Eventually Fettercairn was renovated and the number of stills doubled to four. Whyte & Mackay are the present owners and the malt is distributed by their subsidiary, Invergordon Distillers. Old Fettercairn was once filled into a tiny phial which is recorded in the *Guinness Book of Records* as the smallest bottle of whisky in the world.

Officially available as: 10 years, 26 years Stillman's Dram

Suggested time to serve: Before or after dinner

Tasting notes
Tasted: 10 years—43 percent (Distillery label)
Nose: Faintly caramely with a slight rubbery aroma
Palate: Pleasantly creamy in the mouth with some spicy and smoky dryness
Finish: Fairly light and dry, but warm and lingering

the Stillman's Dram

N° 001581
BOTTLE NUMBER

OLD FETTERCAIRN

AGED **26** YEARS

SINGLE HIGHLAND MALT SCOTCH WHISKY

DISTILLED, AGED AND
BOTTLED IN SCOTLAND
F E T T E R C A I R N
D I S T I L L E R Y
FETTERCAIRN, SCOTLAND

PRODUCT OF SCOTLAND

70cl   45%Vol

Old Pulteney

Region: Northern Highland
Map Ref: 36
Owners: Inverhouse Distillers Ltd.
Address: Huddard Street, Wick, Caithness, KW1 5BA
Telephone: 44 (0)1955 602371
Status: Operational, visiting by appointment

Pulteney Distillery is situated in the fishing town of Wick, just a few miles south of John O'Groats on the north-east coast and has the distinction of being the northernmost operation on the Scottish mainland. The town grew up around the herring industry and for a time prohibition was imposed upon the unruly population, who must have been galled to see the distillery continuing to operate while they dried out.

Pulteney whisky was marketed under the Henderson name for many years. James Henderson opened the distillery in 1826 and his family retained control for over a century. The distillery was recently acquired by Inverhouse Distillers, who have released an official version, the first for many years.

Pulteney whisky is noted as one of the fastest maturing, making it useful to blenders. It has also earned the nickname "The Manzanilla of the North" due to its coastal, salty tang which is reminiscent of a particular style of sherry. There is also a peaty element which translates from Pulteney's water source. The distillery has two small stills and has been much modernized in recent years.

Officially available as: 12 years, 15 years cask strength

Suggested time to serve: Before dinner

Tasting notes
Tasted: 12 years—40 percent (Distillery label)
Nose: Faintly peaty with a refreshing salty aroma
Palate: A little sherry and a little salt. Fairly light in the mouth but smooth and faintly nutty
Finish: Quite long and appetizingly dry

Rosebank

Region: Lowland
Map Ref: 36
Owners: United Distillers
Address: Camelon, Falkirk, Stirlingshire, FK1 5BW
Telephone: 44 (0)1324 623325
Status: Non-operational, not open to visitors

Rosebank Distillery sits alongside the Forth-Clyde Canal at Camelon, near Falkirk. When Rosebank halted production in 1993, Dumbarton-based Auchentoshan (see page 14) became sole survivor of the triple-distilling process in Scotland. It can only be hoped that this great Lowland whisky does not suffer the same fate as its nearest neighbor, St. Magdalene (Linlithgow) which closed for good in 1983.

Rosebank was first produced in the 1840s by James Rankine—ironic that such a name should be shared with my childhood dentist near Glasgow, a man whose drilling first made me crave the soothing influence of whisky! In 1864 Rankine the distiller (not the driller) passed Rosebank to his son who rebuilt the operation and its produce increased in popularity during the boom years of the late 1800s.

Troubled times in the early 1900s forced an amalgamation with Scottish Malt Distillers who evolved to become today's United Distillers. U.D. still own the distillery but there is no certainty as to its future. The malt is highly regarded by connoisseurs and has long epitomized the Lowland style of single malt whisky. It would be a sad loss to the distilling heritage of the area if it were not to reopen.

Officially available as: 12 years, 1981 limited cask strength release

Suggested time to serve: Before dinner

Tasting notes
Tasted: 12 years—43 percent (Distillery label)
Nose: Fresh and dry with a creamy herby fragrance
Palate: Well-balanced and smooth, heading for dryness
Finish: Drying with a slightly acidic citrus feel, though perfectly elegant

LOWLAND
SINGLE MALT
SCOTCH WHISKY

Established on its present
site at *CAMELON* in 1840

ROSEBANK

distillery stands on the
banks of the *FORTH*
and *CLYDE CANAL*.
This was once
a busy thoroughfare with
boats and steamers
continually passing by;
it is still the source
of water for cooling.
This single *MALT
SCOTCH WHISKY* is
triple distilled which
accounts for its *light
distinctive nose* and *well
balanced* flavour.

AGED **12** YEARS

Distilled & Bottled in *SCOTLAND*.
ROSEBANK DISTILLERY
Falkirk, Stirlingshire, Scotland

43% vol 70cl

Royal Lochnagar

Region: Eastern Highland
Map Ref: 38
Owners: United Distillers
Address: Crathie, Ballater, Aberdeenshire, AB35 5TB
Telephone: 44 (0)1339 742273
Status: Operational, open to visitors

Queen Victoria may not have been amused when John Begg invited her to sample his Lochnagar whisky in 1848. His distillery near the Balmoral Estate on Deeside had only been going for three years, and yet Begg was confident enough that his whisky was fit for royalty. The Queen, Prince Albert, and entourage visited the distillery, sampled the wares and granted a royal warrant. John Brown, the Queen's confidant and security specialist, was also a great fan of this dram; on one occasion he is reported to have over-indulged and fell flat on is face in front of Victoria, who quipped that she too had felt an earth tremor.

Lochnagar is not a loch, but the mountain which provides water for the distillery. The first producer on the site was an illicit distiller named James Robertson, who incurred the wrath of his neighbors when he broke with convention and took out an official licence. His distillery was suspiciously burned down in 1841 but was rebuilt and operated for a few years adjacent to John Begg's newer set-up.

In 1880 Henry Begg inherited his father's company and it was retained by the family until 1916 when D.C.L bought it. Lochnagar is one of the smallest distilleries in the Highlands, but is beautifully kept and has an excellent reception center and restaurant.

Officially available as: 12 years, selected reserve, 23 years Rare Malts selection cask strength

Suggested time to serve: After dinner

Tasting notes
Tasted: 12 years—40 percent (Distillery label).
Nose: Soft and honeyed with butterscotch/light caramel and a little smokiness.
Palate: Silky smooth, with a pleasing malty sweetness balancing the smoky element
Finish: Ending sweet with occasional visits of smokiness

AGED YEARS
SINGLE MALT

❦ ROYAL ❦
LOCHNAGAR
Single Highland Malt
SCOTCH WHISKY
❦ Produced in Scotland ❦
BY
Royal Lochnagar Distillery

CRATHIE, DEESIDE
ABERDEENSHIRE
SCOTLAND

40 % vol   70 cl e

ESTP   1845

BY APPOINTMENT TO THEIR LATE MAJESTIES
QUEEN VICTORIA, KING EDWARD VII & KING GEORGE V

The Singleton of Auchroisk

Region: Speyside
Map Ref: 39
Owners: I.D.V. Ltd.
Address: Mulben, Banffshire, AB55 3XS
Telephone: 44 (0)1542 860333
Status: Operational, visiting by appointment

During the 1960s Justerini & Brooks, owners of the famous J&B blended whisky, discovered a particularly good source of soft water emanating from a hillside spring near the Burn of Mulben. The source, known as Dorie's Well, was purchased by the company, along with surrounding land. A protective housing was built over the well and plans were laid for the building of a new distillery, which was finally completed in 1974.

Auchroisk is pronounced "Othrusk" from the Gaelic meaning "the forest of the red stream." The distillery buildings occupy a clearing in the forested hills between the towns of Aberlour and Keith. The bottled single malt became available only as recently as 1986, and has already won many awards gaining worldwide recognition. A decision to introduce the whisky as The Singleton (meaning single malt) was wisely taken, although the Auchroisk part of the name gets easier after a couple of glasses.

Officially available as: 10 years

Suggested time to serve: After dinner

Tasting notes
Tasted: 10 years—40 percent (Distillery label)
Nose: Slightly sweet with pronounced cereal and maltiness, plus some sherry and spice
Palate: Full, almost enveloping, and an initial slight green astringency subsides to reveal pleasant spice
Finish: Long and spicy with a lingering sherry flavor and a little drying smoke

Springbank

Region: Campbeltown
Map Ref: 40
Owners: J. & A. Mitchell & Co. Ltd.
Address: Longrow, Campbeltown, Argyll,
PA28 6ET
Telephone: 44 (0)1586 552085
Status: Operational, visiting by appointment

The Mitchell family were practising the illicit craft prior to 1828 when their Springbank Distillery was built. The operation remains in the ownership of direct descendants to this day, having survived the great Campbeltown slump which saw the closure of over 30 neighboring businesses between 1880 and 1930. Now only two exist, the second being Glen Scotia, although Springbank manages to keep alive the name of Longrow, meaning an "old distillery," the site of which forms part of the present warehouse accommodation. Longrow whisky is made in a separate process using Springbank's stills and is much peatier in character than its sister malt.

The stills at Springbank are unusual in setup. There are three in place, two wash and one spirit, with some of the resulting spirit being triple-distilled. There is an antique feel about Springbank's equipment and all of the traditional whisky making processes are carried out by the staff, including peat cutting, malting, and even bottling. The end product is a whisky of outstanding quality and character—truly one of Scotland's greatest and a personal favorite.

Officially available as: C.V. (Chairman's Vatting), 12 years, 21 years and vintage specials

Suggested time to serve: After dinner

Tasting notes
Tasted: 21 years—46 percent (Distillery label)
Nose: A combination of salt and sherry with a little sweetness
Palate: Creamy and oily, remarkably smooth with waves of saltiness
Finish: Long, rich, and balanced

SPRINGBANK

AGED
21
YEARS

AGED
21
YEARS

ESTABLISHED 1828

CAMPBELTOWN

Scotch **SINGLE MALT** Whisky

PRODUCT OF SCOTLAND

Distilled by J. & A. MITCHELL & CO. LTD.
Springbank Distillery · Campbeltown · Scotland

70cl   46% vol

Strathisla

Region: Speyside
Map Ref: 41
Owners: The Seagram Company Ltd.
Address: Seafield Avenue, Keith, Banffshire, AB55 3BS
Telephone: 44 (0)1542 783042
Status: Operational, open to visitors

Strathisla, on the River Isla in Keith, began its life as a flax mill and was converted for distilling purposes as early as 1786, making it one of Scotland's oldest operations. It probably has also one of the prettiest set of buildings, with its ornate pagoda roofs and old watermill. The distillery was originally known as Milltown, later becoming Milton, a name which it kept until the 1950s when the current owners, Seagrams, gave it its present title. The whisky had been marketed locally as Strathisla since the late 1800s and Elgin merchants, Gordon & MacPhail, were given a concession to buy and mature stocks which they sold further afield.

Prior to the takeover by Chivas brothers in 1950, the company was in receivership, its owner at the time, Jay Pomeroy, was found to have been supplying non-existent companies in London with his wares. The whisky was actually sold to black marketeers and Pomeroy was eventually prosecuted for tax evasion amounting to over £110,000. Strathisla's sister distillery, Glen Keith, is situated on the opposite bank of the River Isla. Both whiskies contribute to Chivas brothers blends.

Officially available as: 12 years

Suggested time to serve: After dinner

Tasting notes
Tasted: 12 years—43 percent (Distillery label)
Nose: Quite assertive, some nectary fruit, and balancing oakiness
Palate: Rounded, at first malty, fruity-sweet and then drying with a firm wood spice
Finish: Long, smoky with a little bitter chocolate character

Strathisla Distillery KEITH - Scotland. Estd 1786

"STRATHISLA"
PURE HIGHLAND MALT
SCOTCH WHISKY
THE OLDEST DISTILLERY IN THE HIGHLANDS

AGED **12** YEARS

70 cl ℮

DISTILLED AND BOTTLED BY CHIVAS BROTHERS LTD
STRATHISLA DISTILLERY, KEITH, AB55 5BS, SCOTLAND

43% vol

Talisker

Region: Islands
Map Ref: 42
Owners: United Distillers
Address: Carbost, Isle of Skye, IV47 8SR
Telephone: 44 (0)1478 640203
Status: Operational, open to visitors

Skye is an island of legends, and indeed its single distillery at Carbost on the shore of Loch Harport, produces a legendary single malt. Talisker's fame is affirmed in numerous pieces of literature, including Robert Louis Stevenson's poem, from 1880, "The Scotsman's Return from Abroad," part of which runs, "The King of drinks as I conceive it, Talisker, Islay or Glenlivet."

The distillery was constructed by the Macaskill brothers in 1843, but only once they had cleared the land of crofters and profited from sheep farming. In 1892, Alexander Allan took control at Talisker and merged it with Dailuaine Distillery on Speyside. Both distilleries were absorbed by The Distillers Company in 1925. Talisker was once triple-distilled, but is now produced in the more conventional manner. In 1960 the stillhouse caught fire, destroying all five stills. Exact copies were made and the quality of the whisky has not suffered.

Skye was once accessible only by ferry, but recently a bridge has been built to the mainland making distillery visits more feasible.

Officially available as: 10 years

Suggested time to serve: After dinner

Tasting notes
Tasted: 10 years—45.8 percent (Distillery label)
Nose: Assertive, pungent, and malty-sweet
Palate: Big, fat, and oily with burnt, peat flavors
Finish: Long and peppery with a little residual sweetness to calm the smoke

ISLE OF SKYE

TALISKER

SINGLE MALT SCOTCH WHISKY

Beyond Carbost Village
close to the Shore is a
gentle haven sheltered
from the bleak ravenes
which sweep down to
the coast.
Here in the shadow of the
distant Cuillin Hills lies
the islands only distillery
Talisker.
The Golden Spirit of Skye
has more than a hint of
local seaweed peppered
with sour & sweet notes
and a memorable warm
peaty finish.

45.8% vol | TALISKER DISTILLERY CARBOST SKYE | 70 cl

ESTABLISHED
1830
TALISKER
DISTILLERY
ISLE OF SKYE

Tomatin

Region: Northern Highland
Map Ref: 43
Owners: Takara Shuzo & Okura & Co. Ltd.
Address: Tomatin, Inverness-shire, IV13 7YT
Telephone: 44 (0)1808 511444
Status: Operational, open to visitors

Fifteen miles or so up the main A9 road from Aviemore to Inverness is situated one of Scotland's largest distilling operations. Tomatin sits high up on exposed moorland close to the point where the River Findhorn meets the Allt-na-Frithe, the "Free Burn" which provides Tomatin's soft water. The burn runs off the Monadhliath Mountains, crossing peat and granite before reaching the distillery.

Tomatin was built 100 years ago with a two-still configuration, and this remained the case until 1956 when the first of many expansions took place. Much of Tomatin's output contributes to the blended market, a factor which was critical when the market slumped in the 1980s and the company failed. In 1986 the distillery was rescued by a Japanese partnership, which has continued to invest in modernization. Tomatin now has 23 stills and enough mechanical and electronic gadgetry to ensure that two people can oversee the entire distillation process.

Scotland's distillers are capable of diverse initiatives and experiments have taken place recently to utilize warm waste water from the plant to raise eels and trout in tanks. There is, however, nothing fishy about the quality of Tomatin malt whisky.

Officially available as: 10 years

Suggested time to serve: Before dinner

Tasting notes
Tasted: 10 years—43 percent (Distillery label)
Nose: Clean and light with a little caramel sweetness
Palate: Quite light, building a little with some smoke and spice
Finish: A good, slightly peppery, spicy finish

Visiting Distilleries

I have attempted to indicate which distilleries are able to cater for visitors. However, please remember that situations do change from time to time and most distilleries have annual periods of closure. To be on the safe side, telephone ahead to establish opening times, tour durations and the numbers catered for. Although it is always tempting to try a whisky where it is made, please be reminded that drinking and driving do not mix. Some distilleries will offer a complimentary miniatures and others have excellent shops where you can buy a bottle or two to take home.

Bibliography and Further Reading

Arthur, Helen; *The Single Malt Whisky Companion*; Apple.

Brander, Michael; *The Essential Guide to Scotch Whisky*; Canongate.

Brown, Gordon; *The Whisky Trails*; Prion.

Cooper, Derek; *A Taste of Scotch*; Andre Deutsch.

Daiches, David; *Scotch Whisky, Its Past and Present*; Fontana.

Lamond and Turer; *The Malt File*; The Edinburgh Publishing Co. Ltd.

Jackson, Michael; *The World Guide to Whisky*; Dorling Kindersley.

Jackson, Michael; *Malt Whisky Companion*; Dorling Kindersley.

Maclean, Charles; *Pocket Whisky Book*; Mitchell Beazley.

Milroy, Wallace; *The Malt Whisky Almanac*, 6th edition; Neil Wilson Publishing.

Skipworth, Mark; *The Scotch Whisky Book*; Lomond Books.

List of other Distilleries

Aberfeldy	S. Highland	Glenesk	E. Highland
Allt A Bhainne	Speyside	Glenglassaugh	Speyside
An Cnoc	Speyside	Glen Keith	Speyside
Ardmore	Speyside	Glenlochy	W. Highland
Arran	Islands	Glenlossie	Speyside
Aultmore	Speyside	Glentauchers	Speyside
		Glenugie	E. Highland
Balblair	N. Highland	Glenury Royal	E. Highland
Balmenach	Speyside		
Banff	E. Highland	Imperial	Speyside
Ben Nevis	W. Highland	Inchgower	Speyside
Benriach	Speyside	Inchmurrin	S. Highland
Benrinnes	Speyside	Inverleven	Lowland
Benromach	Speyside		
Bladnoch	Lowland	Kinclaith	Lowland
Blair Atholl	S. Highland	Kininvie	Speyside
Braes og Glenlivet	Speyside		
Brora	N. Highland	Littlemill	Lowland
		Lochside	E. Highland
Caol Ila	Islay	Longrow	Campbeltown
Caperdonich	Speyside		
Coleburn	Speyside	Macduff	Speyside
Convalmore	Speyside	Mosstowie	Speyside
Craigellachie	Speyside		
		Northport	E. Highland
Dailulaine	Speyside		
Dallas Dhu	Speyside	Old Rhosdhu	S. Highland
Deanston	S. Highland		
Drumguish	N. Highland	Port Ellen	Islay
Dufftown	Speyside		
Glen Albyn	N. Highland	Royal Brackla	N. Highland
Glenallachie	Speyside		
Glenburgie	Speyside	Scapa	Island
Glencadam	Speyside	Speyburn	Speyside
Glencraig	Speyside	St Magdalene	Lowland
Glen Deveron	Speyside		
Glendronach	Speyside	Tamnavulin	Speyside
Glendullan	Speyside	Teaninich	N. Highland
Glen Elgin	Speyside	Tormore	Speyside